First published by Parragon in 2007
Parragon
Queen Street House
4 Queen Street
Bath BA1 1HE, UK

www.bratz.com
TM & © MGA Entertainment, Inc.
"Bratz", and all related logos, names,
characters and distinctive likenesses are the
exclusive property of MGA Entertainment, Inc.
All Rights Reserved. Used under license by Parragon.

ISBN 978-1-4054-9161-7

Printed in China

THE KITTYNAPPER

PaRragon
Bath New York Singapore Hong Kong Cologne Delhi Melbourne

Jade and Micah are totally runway-ready.

Cloe's sneezing fit continues.

Ah-choo! Ah-choo!

Jade, your cat is so stylin'.

And so perfect for my article, 'What Your Pet Says About You.'

Chachi's dog, Joni, doesn't like Micah.

GRRRRRRR!!

Micah doesn't like Joni much either!

Meow!! Hisss!!

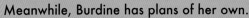

Meanwhile, Burdine has plans of her own.

We just have to beat Chachi and his miserable little mutt this year. Especially after last year...

Burdine remembers her ruined acceptance speech.

Chachi unleashed the hounds. Well, one hound. A really small dog, actually. But with sharp teeth.

Burdine was NOT pleased.

Mother of pink!

Burdine tried to exit the stage gracefully, but it was hard with only half a dress.

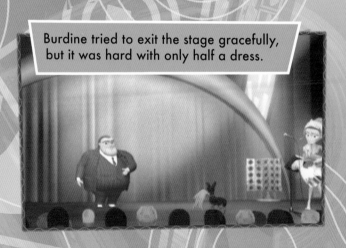

The Tweevils try to capture Micah.

Come on! Let's get her!

Micah is too fast and the Tweevils take a tumble.

Kaycee pulls Micah off her.

Kaycee dances away, happy she got an apology out of her sister.

The kitty is finally kittynapped!

The Bratz get to work on a cat-finding crusade.

Sasha takes photocopies to hand out.

Jade puts Micah's image on balloons and ties them around town.

Cloe puts up the last stylin' Micah flyer.

Jade hears more bad news from Chachi.

I'm so sorry! Bye!

Joni's missing too! What if I never see Micah again?

Kirstee, where do they get that saying, 'fight like cats and dogs'?

Hmmm. I think it's because dogs and cats, like, fight so much.

Really? Let's see!

Kaycee puts Royale in Micah's cage.

After the Tweevils leave, a stranger in black heads down the hallway.

Micah hates this new visitor even more than Royale.

HISSSSSSSS!!!!!!!!!

The sinister stranger approaches the cage.

The pathetic petnapper keeps running.

Cloe!

Cloe chases after until she meets a little obstacle.

Oh my gosh! Are you okay?!

Cloe is fine, just annoyed the petnapper escaped. But she still has a clue...

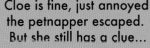

Cameron pulls up to see what the problem is.

Fix my flat and I'll make it well worth your while.

That's not just a flat. Somebody slashed your tyre.

Cameron gets off his bike and takes a closer look.

Burdine has plenty of enemies, but this still comes as a surprise.

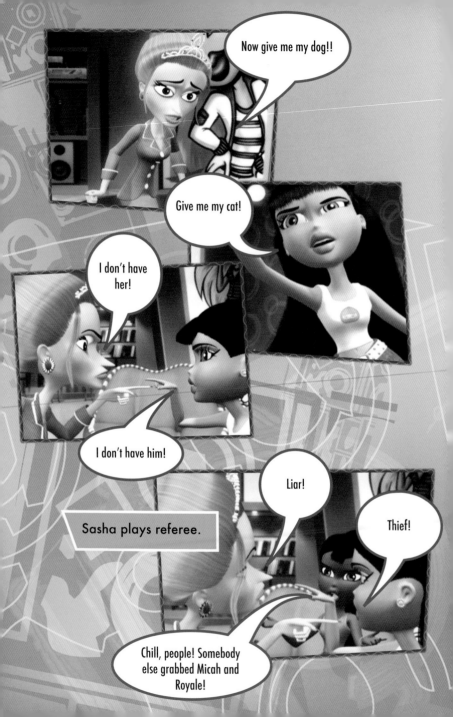

Then Jade sees something strange.

She finds a tuft of pink fur.

Jade lifts the pillow
and looks underneath.

The fabric under the pillow is the same as the torn piece of blanket. Something funny is going on.

Chachi looks a little shifty.

Jade decides to get out of there, pronto.

Well, call us if you hear anything.

Cameron gets ready to ride.

I gotta get over there!

Sasha works her phone finger.

I'm getting the police!

Ahhhh!

Jade isn't a big rat fan either.

Shhhh!!!!

Oh my gosh! I hear them!

Jade opens the cage and Micah jumps in her arms.

I never want to let you go!

Burdine and Royale are reunited as well.

Oh! Royale!

The reunion is everything Burdine dreamed of. Sort of.

The food processor looks super-scary.

Burdine and Royale don't like the sound of that.

The cans are pretty, but the contents taste awful.

Burdine and Jade try to make a break for it.

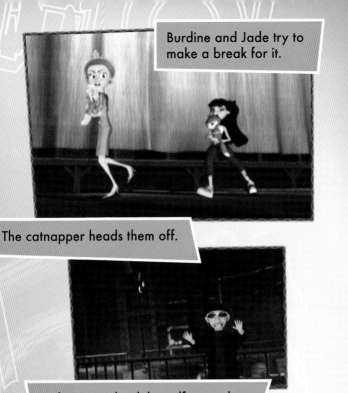

The catnapper heads them off.

Jade tries to hook herself a crook.

But the catnapper is as quick as a cat.

Cameron takes matters into his own feet.

We'll see who's chopped liver!

Cameron hears Jade calling for help.

Later, at the pet show...

Let's hear it for Royale and his owner, Burdine Maxwell!

Can you believe that Burdine was, like, able to bribe all the judges again this year?

I know, she's such a people person.

The judge is a little surprised.

Huh? I can't believe it. Burdine Maxwell and Royale?

The crowd is shocked and showers the judges with more boos.

What?!

There's got to be a mistake!

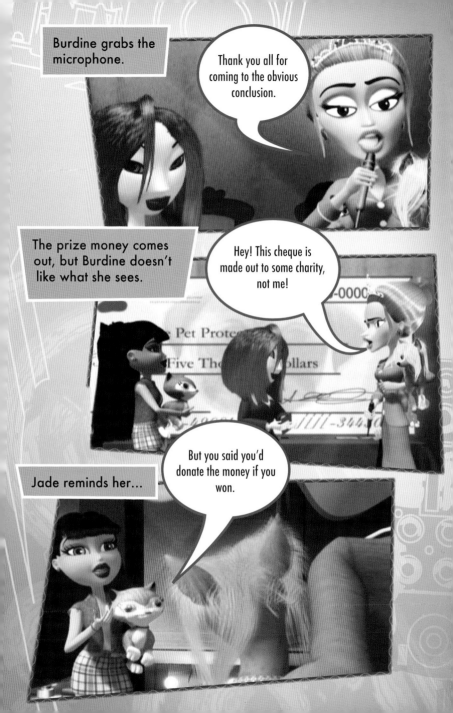

BRATZ™

YASMIN™

Sometimes Yasmin can be a little quiet, but even without her saying a word, you can sense this girl's special. There's just something about her that seems almost regal. But Yasmin's not pretentious! She's really open-minded – she's always up on alternative trends in fashion, fitness and beauty!
Nickname: Pretty Princess

SASHA™

Sasha's not afraid of confrontation – she knows who she is, what she wants and how to get it! Fashion's a huge part of her life, but music is even more important to 'Bunny Boo!' Someday you can be sure she'll be a record producer... with her own fashion line!
Nickname: Bunny Boo

JADE™

Always on the cutting edge of cool, Jade's the ultimate fashionista! After checking out the latest fashion mags, the trendiest boutiques and all the thrift stores, she always manages to put together looks that are completely unique and just scream 'Kool Kat!'
Nickname: Kool Kat

CLOE™

Cloe's so creative that her whole life has become a work of art, from designing fantastic fashions to creating cool new cosmetic looks to her tendency to be dramatic! Sometimes her imagination runs away with her, but her friends help this 'Angel' stay grounded!
Nickname: Angel